photo word book

Vegetables

Camilla Lloyd

WAYLAND

zwijsen
bdyslexie
font
is the typeface used in this book

First published in 2014 by Wayland
Copyright © Wayland 2014

Wayland
338 Euston Road
London NW1 3BH

Wayland Australia
Level 17/207 Kent Street
Sydney, NSW 2000

Editor: Elizabeth Brent
Designer: Amy McSimpson

Dewey number: 428.1-dc23

ISBN   978 0 7502 8293 2
eBook ISBN   978 0 7502 8525 4

Printed in China

10 9 8 7 6 5 4 3 2 1

Picture acknowledgements: All images, including the cover image, courtesy of Shutterstock.com,
except: p4–5 © valentinrussanov/iStockPhoto, p11 © Tanya Constantine/Blend Images/Corbis,
p22 © Wiktory/iStockPhoto

Wayland is a division of Hachette Children's Books, an Hachette UK company.
www.hachette.co.uk

Contents

vegetables

These are vegetables.

Eating vegetables
is very good for you.

carrots

These are carrots.

Carrots grow in the ground.

cucumbers

This is a cucumber.

Inside a cucumber there are soft seeds.

lettuces

This is a lettuce.

Lettuces have crispy green leaves.

9

broccoli

This is broccoli.

Broccoli can be cooked before you eat it.

potatoes

These are potatoes

Potatoes grow underground.

13

sweetcorn

This is **sweetcorn**.

Sweetcorn grows on a hard core called a cob.

14

peas

These are peas.

Peas are small, round and green.

17

celery

This is celery.

Celery is crunchy and tastes nice with cheese.

onions

These are onions.

The inside of an **onion** can be used in cooking.

21

Picture quiz

Can you find out which of these vegetables grow in the ground?

carrots

celery

peas

potatoes

What pages are they on?

22

Index quiz

The index is on page 24.
Use the index to answer these questions.

1. Which pages show **peas**?
   What shape are peas?

2. Which page shows **celery**?
   What does celery taste nice with?

3. Which page shows **sweetcorn**?
   What is the hard core that sweetcorn
   grows on called?

4. Which page shows an **onion**?
   Which part of the onion is used
   in cooking?

Index

Answers

Picture quiz: Potatoes and carrots grow in the ground. The carrots are on pages 6 & 7. The celery is on pages 18 & 19. The peas are on pages 16 & 17. The potatoes are on pages 12 & 13.

Index quiz: 1. Pages 16 & 17, peas are round; 2. Pages 18 & 19, celery tastes nice with cheese; 3. Pages 14 & 15, sweetcorn grows on a cob; 4. Pages 20 & 21, the inside of the onion is used in cooking.